CHATSWORTH

The home of the Duke and Duchess of Devonshire.

Welcome to Chatsworth. My family and I take great pleasure in sharing our home with all our visitors. For centuries, Chatsworth has received guests from all over the world, and everyone who lives and works here is pleased to welcome you today.

I am very proud of all that my family and many generations of estate staff have created here over the last five centuries, handing down a place of great beauty and fascination for all of us to enjoy. I am also excited by the opportunity we have to continue to improve and enhance the house, its collection, landscape and other businesses, striving to make Chatsworth as enjoyable and interesting as possible.

The family's collections have been changing and growing since the 1550s, reflecting the tastes and enthusiasms of each generation. As you walk through the house today, I hope you will enjoy seeing new acquisitions alongside the diverse works of art from the past. Many of my forebears collected the contemporary art of their time, and my wife and I continue this tradition.

Following the detailed agreement of the Peak District National Park Authority, English Heritage and other statutory advisers, we have recently embarked on a masterplan to upgrade all the services in the house, and to make improvements to the route visitors take around the house, which will open new spaces, create new views indoors and outside, and reduce the number of stairs you have to negotiate. You may see masterplan projects taking place today, and I hope you will return in years to come, to see the fruits of this skilled and painstaking work.

This book is an indispensable guide, giving you useful information about the house, its history and the collection. I hope it contributes to you having an inspiring day and that you will come back to see the house and the collection as they continue to change and grow. Thank you for visiting.

Devonshire

The 12th Duke of Devonshire, CBE

A TIMELINE
OF CHATSWORTH & THE CAVENDISH FAMILY

m. (1) Robert Barlow,
(1529–44),
Bess's first husband

m. (2) Sir William Cavendish,
(*c.* 1508–57),
Bess's second husband

Bess of Hardwick
(1521–1608)
The 'first lady of Chatsworth',
Bess of Hardwick grew up in
Derbyshire and, from modest
beginnings, became the
second most powerful woman
in Elizabethan England after the
Queen. She married four times,
but only had children by her
second husband, Sir William
Cavendish. The Cavendish line
established by Bess continues
at Chatsworth
to this day.

Bess of
Hardwick's
silver livery
badge

Elizabethan Chatsworth, by Richard Wilson, (1713–82), after a lost
17th-century original

HARDWICK HALL

Bess's surviving masterpiece is Hardwick Hall, 17 miles (27 km)
from Chatsworth. One of the greatest houses of the Elizabethan age,
it has a fine garden and park and unique collections of 16th- and
17th-century embroideries, tapestries and furniture. It belonged to the
Cavendish family until 1957, when it was given to the government in
lieu of death duties, and is now a National Trust property.

1493 Christopher Colombus
returns from his first voyage
to the 'New World'.

1509 Henry VIII
becomes King

1521 Henry VIII
made 'Defender
of the Faith'

1534 Henry becomes
Supreme Head of the
Church of England

1536 The
Dissolution of the
Monasteries
begins

Mary Queen of Scots was held prisoner at Chatsworth at various times between 1569 and 1584, in the custody of Shrewsbury. The rooms in which she stayed on the east side of the house, though changed beyond recognition, are still called the Queen of Scots Apartments.

m. **(3) Sir William St Loe,** (1518–65), Bess's third husband

m. **(4) George Talbot**, 6th Earl of Shrewsbury, (c. 1528–90), Bess's fourth husband

ELIZABETHAN CHATSWORTH

Bess realised that ownership of land was the best way to establish her family as a powerful dynasty. She persuaded Sir William Cavendish to sell the former monastic lands he had amassed as one of Henry VIII's commissioners for the Dissolution of the Monasteries, and move to her home county. Despite its isolated moorland location, prone to flooding, they bought Chatsworth manor for £600 in 1549, and in 1552 began to build. Almost nothing remains of their large house, which stood surrounding a courtyard with a west-facing gatehouse on the site of the present building. On the hill behind the house, their Hunting Tower survives. It was built in the 1580s as a vantage point from which to view the valley below, or to watch the hunt on the moor behind.

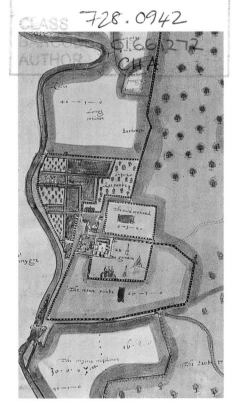

William Senior's map of Chatsworth, 1617

Needlework panel of Chatsworth, c. 1590–1600

1547 Edward VI becomes King

1558 Elizabeth I becomes Queen after Mary I dies

1561 Future James VI of Scotland and James I of England born

1581 Francis Drake is knighted

c. **1598** Inigo Jones first visits Italy and will later introduce Renaissance architecture to England

1600   1610   1620   1630   1640

m. **Hon. Christian Bruce,**
daughter of 1st Lord Kinloss,
a redoubtable character, she
was responsible for the
recovery of the family fortunes
after the extravangances of her
husband

William Cavendish,
(1552–1626), 1st Earl of
Devonshire, (1618–26)

   m. **Anne Keighley,**
daughter of
Henry Keighley

William Cavendish,
(1590–1628),
2nd Earl of Devonshire,
(1626– 28)

The Earls of Devonshire were active members of the Court in London and patrons of artists and writers, and these family traditions have been maintained throughout the centuries. The first Earl invested in America and Bermuda, and the famous philosopher Thomas Hobbes was engaged as tutor to both the 2nd and 3rd Earls.

Bolsover Castle
This 17th-century mansion was built in the style of a medieval castle by Sir Charles Cavendish, son of Bess of Hardwick, and his son William, the 1st Duke of Newcastle.

THE GREAT REBUILDING

Between 1687 and 1707 the 4th Earl (and later 1st Duke) systematically dismantled Bess's Elizabethan house and rebuilt Chatsworth wing by wing. The Duke worked closely with architects William Talman and Thomas Archer to create a house that reflected his own political ambition and importance. The finest of Europe's artists and craftsmen were commissioned to decorate the interiors in the latest baroque style. Its crowning glory was a majestic State Apartment, replacing the Tudor long gallery, fit to receive the new King and Queen. The new house, with its extensive formal gardens, including the Cascade, Canal and Willow Tree Fountain, was barely completed when the Duke died.

Christin in Glory (detail) from Laguerre's painted ceiling in the Chapel, commissioned by the 1st Duke

1600   1610   1620   1630   1640

1603 James I becomes King

1605 Gunpowder Plot

1620 The Pilgrim Fathers depart for America aboard the *Mayflower*

1625 James I dies and Charles I accedes to the throne

1642 The English Civil War begins; Chatsworth is occupied by both sides

William Cavendish,
(1617–84), 3rd Earl
of Devonshire,
(1628–84)

m.

Lady Elizabeth Cecil,
daughter of 2nd Earl
of Salisbury

William Cavendish,
(1641–1707),
4th Earl (1684) and later
1st Duke of Devonshire,
(1694–1707)

m. **Lady Mary Butler,**
daughter of 1st Duke
of Ormonde

Kip and Knyff's engraving of 1699, (detail) showing the house after the 1st Duke had rebuilt the south and east fronts, with some of the new formal garden

1649 Charles I is executed at Whitehall

1658 Oliver Cromwell dies

1665 Great Plague of London begins

1666 Great Fire of London

1688 Glorious Revolution – William and Mary

1697 Ceila Fiennes visits Chatsworth

1700   1710   1720   1730   1740

William Cavendish, (1673–1729), 2nd Duke of Devonshire, (1707–29), a close friend of Prime Minister Sir Robert Walpole, as was his son the 3rd Duke

m. **Hon. Rachel Russell,** daughter of Lord William Russell

William Cavendish, (1698–1755), 3rd Duke of Devonshire, (1729–55). Member of Parliament before entering the House of Lords, and a popular Lord Lieutenant of Ireland for seven years

m. **Katherine Hoskins,** daughter of John Hoskins

The 2nd Duke greatly enhanced the Devonshire Collection which fills the house today, with collections of paintings, drawings, prints, coins and carved Greek and Roman gems. Unusually for his time, he welcomed scholars who wished to see the collections, a tradition that continues today.

Chatsworth c. 1770, by William Marlow, showing Paine's new kitchen wing and the stables, to the left of the house

Portrait of an Oriental by Rembrandt, bought by the 3rd Duke in 1742

Devonshire House
The 3rd Duke commissioned fashionable architect and designer, William Kent, to rebuild Devonshire House in Piccadilly after it burnt down in 1733, and to design its furniture, much of which is now at Chatsworth.

Adoration of the Magi by Paolo Veronese, bought by the 2nd Duke in 1722

1700   1710   1720   1730   1740

1702 William III dies

1710 Sir Christopher Wren's St Paul's Cathedral is completed

1724 Daniel Defoe describes Chatsworth as 'the most pleasant garden and the most beautiful palace in the world'

William Cavendish, (1720–64), 4th Duke of Devonshire, (1755–64), Lord Lieutenant of Ireland and Prime Minister of England between November 1756 and May 1757

m.　**Lady Charlotte Boyle,** daughter of 4th Earl of Cork and 3rd Earl of Burlington. Charlotte died from smallpox at the age of 23

William Cavendish, (1748–1811), 5th Duke of Devonshire, (1764–1811)

m.

(2) Lady Elizabeth Foster, daughter of 1st Earl of Bristol

m.　**(1) Lady Georgiana Spencer,** daughter of 1st Earl Spencer. Georgiana was a celebrated beauty, leader of fashion and radical political canvasser. It was well known that for several years a harmonious *ménage à trois* existed between the Duke and Duchess and their friend, Lady Elizabeth Foster, who went on to become the 5th Duke's second wife after Georgiana's death

18TH-CENTURY CHATSWORTH

The 4th Duke commissioned Lancelot 'Capability' Brown, one of the greatest English landscape gardeners, to create the magnificent park. Much of the 1st Duke's formal garden, and the stables and cottages in Edensor village which interfered with the view to the west, were destroyed to create the illusion of a natural landscape. James Paine (c. 1716–89) was commissioned to build a new wing to the north of the house, as well as a magnificent new stables and the stone bridge which still survive.

Lady Charlotte Boyle was the only surviving child of Richard Boyle, 3rd Earl of Burlington (1694/5–1753), the great Palladian architect and patron of the arts. Her marriage to the 4th Duke united the collections of both families. The Burlington inheritance included 80,000 acres (32,375 hectares) of land across various estates, their houses and their contents, including many of Lord Burlington's architectural books and drawings.

The 5th Duke lived mostly in London, but he and Georgiana received many fashionable guests at Chatsworth. Once a week the house was opened to visitors, who were even provided with dinner and, in 1775, an inn, now the estate office, was built for sightseers at Edensor. John Carr of York (1723–1807) was commissioned by the 5th Duke to create the Crescent in Buxton.

Henry Cavendish, (1731–1810), grandson of the 2nd Duke, was a distinguished and eccentric scientist, and 'the first man to weigh the world'

1750　　　1760　　　1770　　　1780　　　1790

1746 Battle of Culloden

1762 Rousseau's *Social Contract* first published

1770 James Cook discovers New South Wales

1775 Richard Arkwright's waterpower looms used at Cromford textile mills

1776 American Declaration of Independence from Britain

1789 French Revolution begins

7

| 1800 | 1810 | 1820 | 1830 | 1840 |

William Spencer Cavendish, (1790–1858), 6th Duke of Devonshire, (1811–58)

Joseph Paxton (1803–65)
The 'Bachelor' Duke was intensely interested in gardening and, in 1826, appointed the young Joseph Paxton as Chatsworth's head gardener. Through ambitious feats of engineering, including giant rockeries and the gravity-fed Emperor Fountain, they transformed the garden. Paxton also supervised the rebuilding of Edensor village. His reputation was assured with the success of Chatsworth's Great Conservatory and the Crystal Palace in London. He is remembered as one of Victorian England's greatest self-made men.

19TH-CENTURY CHATSWORTH

Extravagant and charming, the 6th 'Bachelor' Duke never married, but loved entertaining guests. Victoria visited twice, as Princess and Queen and, when the Midland Railway reached Rowsley in 1849, 80,000 people visited the house during the summer. The 6th Duke spent 47 years improving his many houses and collecting objects of every kind, particularly books and sculpture. He commissioned the architect Sir Jeffry Wyatville (1766–1840) to modernise many rooms in the old house, and built a new long North Wing with dining room, sculpture gallery, orangery, private theatre and many staff rooms including a new kitchen, other food preparation rooms, a servants' hall and the laundry, which served all the Duke's residences.

Chatsworth in 1828, by William Cowan, showing Wyatville's new north wing

Trial by Jury, by Sir Edwin Landseer, from the 6th Duke's collection

Veiled Vestal Virgin, by Rafaelle Monti, purchased by the 6th Duke in 1848

| 1800 | 1810 | 1820 | 1830 | 1840 |

1804 Trevethick's steam locomotive pulls five wagons and 70 passengers

1812 Jane Austen's *Pride and Prejudice* is first published, with Chatsworth said to be the inspiration for Mr Darcy's mansion, Pemberley

1821 George IV becomes King

1832 Princess Victoria visits Chatsworth, drawing crowds of thousands from across the Peak District

1837 Victoria becomes Queen

William Cavendish, (1808–91), 7th Duke of Devonshire, (1858–91)

m.

Lady Blanche Howard, daughter of 6th Earl of Carlisle

Spencer Compton Cavendish, (1833–1908), 8th Duke of Devonshire, (1891–1908)

m.

Louise von Alten, widow of the Duke of Manchester, 'The Double Duchess'

The 7th Duke was the grandson of the 6th Duke's uncle, Lord George Cavendish. He was Chancellor of London University at the age of 28, and later Chancellor of Cambridge University and founder of its Cavendish Laboratory. The 7th Duke rebuilt Edensor Church, but decreed strict economies at Chatsworth after the extravagance of his predecessor. He is remembered for his urban developments at Eastbourne and Barrow-in-Furness. Granddaughter of Duchess Georgiana, his wife, Blanche, died aged 29 and was mourned by her husband and her uncle for the rest of their lives.

The 8th Duke played a leading role in the cabinets of Gladstone and later led the Liberal government. Three times he was asked by Queen Victoria to become Prime Minister, but each time he refused. In 1886 he split the Liberal party over his opposition to Home Rule for Ireland. He and his wife entertained lavishly at Chatsworth, where King Edward VII and Queen Alexandra were regular visitors.

Paxton's Great Conservatory

The 8th Duke commissioned water power turbines to generate electricity for the house.

1849 The Midland Railway reaches Rowsley, 3 miles (4.8 km) away, and 80,000 people visit the house during the summer

1851 Paxton's Crystal Palace houses the Great Exhibition

1868 William Gladstone becomes Prime Minister for the first time

1896 First motor cars appear on the road

| 1900 | 1910 | 1920 | 1930 | 1940 |

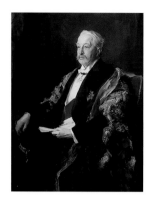

Victor Cavendish, (1868–1938), 9th Duke of Devonshire, (1908–38)

m. **Lady Evelyn Petty Fitzmaurice**, daughter of 5th Marquess of Lansdowne

Edward Cavendish, (1895–1950), 10th Duke of Devonshire, (1938–50)

m. **Lady Mary Cecil**, daughter of 4th Marquess of Salisbury

Chatsworth from the North East

The 9th Duke held offices as Financial Secretary to the Treasury and Governor-General of Canada (1916–21), and enjoyed managing his estates. He built a range of stables at Pilsley, now the Farm Shop, and he and Duchess Evie undertook much-needed restoration work in the house. The 9th Duke was the first to have to pay death duties, amounting to over half a million pounds which, added to a running debt since the failure of the 7th Duke's business ventures and the impact of World War I, forced major sacrifices. Paxton's Great Conservatory was demolished and all the Caxton books and many rare first editions of Shakespeare were sold, as were Devonshire House and Chiswick House in London.

Duchess Evie became very knowledgeable about the collections and their conservation, and ensured the pristine state of many of the objects in the house.

The 10th Duke inherited in 1938. During World War II the house was occupied by 300 pupils and teachers from a girls' boarding school, Penrhos College. The State Rooms and corridors became dormitories and the drawing rooms and larger bedrooms were classrooms, with furniture and pictures stored in the Library and Sculpture Gallery. In 1949, the house was prepared for re-opening to visitors and, in spite of petrol rationing, 105,000 people visited within a year.

| 1900 | 1910 | 1920 | 1930 | 1940 |

1901 Queen Victoria dies and Edward VII becomes King

1908 Visitors to Chatsworth pay an entrance fee for the first time, with all proceeds going to local hospitals

1914 Outbreak of World War I

1928 Women granted equal voting rights to men

1936 World's first TV broadcast by the BBC

1939 World War II begins

William, Marquess of Hartington (1917–44) and **Kathleen Kennedy**, sister of President Kennedy. The 10th Duke's elder son, William, married 'Kick' Kennedy in May 1944. Four months later, he was killed in action in Belgium. Kathleen died in an aeroplane accident in 1948

Andrew Cavendish, (1920–2004), 11th Duke of Devonshire, (1950–2004)   m.   **Hon. Deborah Mitford,** (b. 1920) daughter of 2nd Lord Redesdale

The 11th Duke served in the Coldstream Guards during World War II and won the Military Cross, was Mayor of Buxton between 1952–54 and a minister in the Conservative government of 1960–64. In 1996, the Duke was made a Knight of the Garter. He died in 2004, having held the title for longer than any of his predecessors.

He inherited the estate with 80% death duties which took 24 years to settle. Many important works of art, rare books, thousands of acres of land and Hardwick Hall were sold or given to the nation in lieu of tax. A keen collector of books, minerals and modern British art, the 11th Duke and his wife led a revival of Chatsworth's fortunes in the second half of the 20th century.

The Farmyard was opened in 1973, to offer an entertaining but realistic explanation of the life cycles and ultimate uses of the commercial farm stock on the estate. The Farm Shop in Pilsley village, 1.5 miles (2.4 km) from Chatsworth, opened in 1977, focusing on Chatsworth produce, such as meat, game, dairy products and potatoes. It has since expanded and now sells British food and wines, as well as hosting food tastings, talks and demonstrations.

Large interior, W9, 1973, by Lucian Freud

THE CHATSWORTH HOUSE TRUST

In 1981, the charitable Chatsworth House Trust was set up by the 11th Duke to ensure the long-term survival of the house and collection for the benefit of visitors. Since 1949, the entrance money paid by more than 20 million visitors has made a vital contribution to the maintenance of the house, garden and park. The Duke of Devonshire and his family pay rent to live in part of the house and manage Chatsworth with the support of the Trust's Council of Management.

Georgiana Duchess of Devonshire, by Thomas Gainsborough, purchased by the Chatsworth House Trust in 1994

1951 Festival of Britain opened by George VI

1952 Elizabeth II becomes Queen

1964 First Beatles tour of the USA

1969 First man lands on the moon

1979 Margaret Thatcher becomes Britain's first woman Prime Minister

1982 Falklands War

1989 World Wide Web invented

2000   **2010**   **2020**

William Cavendish, (b.1969), Earl of Burlington

m. Laura Montagu, (b.1972), daughter of Richard Roundell

Peregrine Cavendish, (b.1944), 12th Duke of Devonshire since 2004

m. Amanda Heywood-Lonsdale, (b.1944), daughter of Commander Edward Heywood-Lonsdale RN

CHATSWORTH TODAY

As well as Chatsworth, the current Duke manages the family estates at Bolton Abbey in Yorkshire and elsewhere. He is The Queen's Representative and Chairman of Ascot Racecourse and Deputy Chairman of Sotheby's. He is a trustee of Sheffield Museums and Galleries Trust, the Wallace Collection, the Storm King Art Center (USA) and in late 2008 becomes Chancellor of Derby University.

The Duke and Duchess have one son, William (b. 1969), two daughters, Celina (b. 1971) and Jasmine (b. 1973), and seven grandchildren.

The Duke and Duchess and their son, Lord Burlington, are keen collectors, and you will see works of art they have added to the collection both indoors and outside. The family and the Trust add to the collection with pieces that have a historic link to Chatsworth, or reflect the taste of the current generations, complementing the existing collection or taking it in new directions. Some parts of the collection, particularly drawings, prints and books, cannot often be displayed due to their fragility, but they can be studied by scholars, by prior arrangement. Every year, many objects are lent to different exhibitions around the world, to be seen and enjoyed by a wider audience. In recent years, important contemporary sculptures, a particular interest of the Duke and Duchess, have been installed in the garden and park at Chatsworth, and internationally significant outdoor exhibitions of monumental sculpture are becoming a tradition.

2000

12

The Chatsworth team

Chatsworth has a tradition of long service. In 1963, the 11th Duke gave a party for people who had worked on the Derbyshire estate for 25 years or longer. 175 people came, of whom 123 had done 25 years or more, and 52 had completed over 40 years. Since then, awards have been given at the annual staff party. By 2008 there had been 238 people who had worked for 25 years and 117 for 40 years. Pictured left, the 2008 awards with the Duke and Duchess (centre), the Dowager Duchess (front row, centre) and Lord and Lady Burlington (front row, right).

The masterplan

2008 saw the start of work on a long term house masterplan. Informed by painstaking research and analysis, this work will ensure that the building's services are up-to-date. It also encompasses improvements to the visitor route in the house, including fewer stairs and a new gallery on the second floor, and extensive stonework conservation.

Below: The recently uncovered cascade in Quebec, a 4-acre area of the garden opened in 2008
Bottom: The Duke and Duchess with Allen Jones during the installation of his sculpture, *Déjeuner sur l'herbe*

Chatsworth has recently starred as a location for major films, including *Pride and Prejudice* (2004), *The Duchess* (2008) (shown here: the Duchess with Keira Knightley and Dominic Cooper) and *The Wolf Man* (2009).

THE APPROACH

The approach to the house is under the arch of the Porter's Lodge between an avenue of tulip trees (*Liriodendron tulipifera*), with the long wing, added 1820–27, on your left. This massive building, including the high tower or belvedere above the Theatre at its north end, was built for the 6th 'Bachelor' Duke (1790–1858) by Sir Jeffry Wyatville (1766–1840). It contained the offices, kitchens, laundry, servants' hall, lamp room, still room, boiler room, carpenter's shop, many bedrooms, the Great Dining Room, Sculpture Gallery, Orangery, Theatre and plunge bath. Whilst many of these rooms have changed their use over the last 160 years, it is still the 'engine room' of the house where many of the day-to-day tasks of essential upkeep and maintenance take place. This new North Wing replaced an earlier range of service buildings built about 100 years earlier for the 4th Duke, when he changed the approach to the house with a new bridge erected further up river.

Transplanting mature specimen trees and plants became extremely fashionable in the 19th century, and the weeping ash on the mound opposite the front door was brought from a Derby garden in 1830, when it was already over 40 years old. It forms the centrepiece of the 6th Duke's sweeping carriage drive, which used to pass under a wooden *porte cochère* over the doors, to enable guests to alight from their carriages under cover.

Above: Detail from an architectural drawing by Sir Jeffry Wyatville, *c.* 1820, showing the original shape of the windows on the bow of the North Front, as designed by Thomas Archer in 1705. Wyatville altered the windows for the 6th Duke in the 1830s
Below: Queen Victoria arriving at Chatsworth in 1843
Below right: The North Front today

THE NORTH FRONT HALL

In the 1st Duke's house, this room was the kitchen, the original entrance being at the centre of the the west façade of the building. Having radically changed the approach and moved the kitchens into a new North Wing, the 4th Duke and his architect, James Paine (1716–89) were able to convert this room into a spacious and elegant hall.

The four columns are a copy of one in the gardens of Chiswick House in London, built by the father of the 4th Duke's wife, Lady Charlotte Boyle. Chiswick came into the ownership of the Dukes of Devonshire as a result of Charlotte's inheritance. The staircase and fireplaces were altered for the 6th Duke by Wyatville in 1823–4. It has often been said that the original kitchen ranges survive behind the fireplaces, although no evidence of this has ever been found.

The marble group of a mother and a daughter, and the full-length figure of a man, are Roman, 1st century AD. They were discovered at Apt in Provence and bought by the 6th Duke, a passionate collector of sculpture. The ceiling painting depicts Aurora and is an early 19th-century copy by Amelia Curran (1775–1847) of the original by Guido Reni.

The painting above the fireplace on the right of the entrance shows Bolton Abbey in olden times and was commissioned by the 6th Duke from one of his favourite painters, Sir Edwin Landseer (1803–73). Bolton Abbey is the family's Yorkshire estate, and this romanticised scene imagines what it might have been like before the Dissolution of the Monasteries.

Mother and Daughter,
Roman, 1st century AD

THE NORTH CORRIDOR

This passage was originally an open colonnade through which visitors entered via the west front when it was too wet to walk across the grand inner courtyard. The 6th Duke enclosed it and, in 1841, the coloured marble pavement was laid to disguise the irregular alignment of the windows and doorways. When first laid '…so brightly was it polished it was difficult to make anybody walk on it', he wrote. The mahogany chairs and settees were designed by William Kent (1685–1748) for Chiswick House and Devonshire House in London. On the walls are small paintings by lesser masters of the 17th century, some of which also came from Chiswick.

Part of the coloured marble pavement, 1841, (below) 'by Leonardi, a poor man who lives at the Forum in Rome'

Hall chair, mahogany, designed by William Kent (1685–1748), *c.* 1730

THE PAINTED HALL

The upper part of the Painted Hall has not changed since it was painted in 1692–94 with scenes from the life of Julius Caesar by Louis Laguerre (1663–1721). By contrast, the ground floor and staircase have been altered several times. The marble floor replaced stone in 1779, relaid again for the 6th Duke in 1834. He also inserted three French windows into the courtyard in the 1820s, replacing a painted wainscot along the west wall. The most major changes, however, involved the staircase, which has been rebuilt twice.

Above: *Head of Hermes*, Roman, 2nd century AD, marble Below: Detail of the painted ceiling, showing the apotheosis of Julius Caesar as a demi-god

The original staircase was a double curved flight, rising to the central arch that gives onto the landing of the Great Stairs above. A magnificent piece of architecture, the sides were faced with carved alabaster, and the steps themselves had risers of the local mineral Blue John, creating spectacular effects when lit by candlelight. This was removed for the 6th Duke by the architect Sir Jeffry Wyatville (1766–1840), who designed a single flight and matching galleries along the east and west walls in 1833. This scheme was demolished and replaced by the present stairs and single gallery, designed by W. H. Romaine-Walker for the 9th Duke of Devonshire in 1912. The gilt ironwork was copied from the balustrade wrought

(1689) by the French smith, Jean Tijou, on the Great Stairs above, leading to the second floor.

Three of the four flower paintings are probably by a follower of Jean-Baptiste Monnoyer (1636–99); the fourth is signed by Jakob Bogdany (1660–1724).

Over the fireplace, the 6th Duke's Latin inscription, translated, reads: 'William Spencer Duke of Devonshire inherited this most beautiful house from his father in the year 1811, which had been begun in the year of English liberty 1688, and completed in the year of his bereavement 1840'. The bereavement refers to the early death of his beloved niece, Blanche, Countess of Burlington, the wife of his heir.

In 1936, there was nearly a disaster here. The ceiling was discovered to be sagging and on the point of collapsing onto the floor 29 ft (8.8 metres) below. It took two years to make it safe and, during the summers, visitors had to make their way through a forest of scaffolding poles. In 1996 the ceiling painting was restored followed by the painted walls in 2005–6.

Above: Wrought iron balcony on the west wall of the courtyard, after Jean Tijou (active 1689–1712)
Left: *The Staircase in the Painted Hall*, 1827, detail from watercolour by William Henry Hunt, (1790–1864) showing the original twin curved stairs built for the 1st Duke

20

THE GREAT STAIRS

In a truly baroque house, the State Apartments would have been on this, the first floor, but because Chatsworth was rebuilt piecemeal at the end of the 17th century, it essentially follows the form of an Elizabethan house. As a result, the grandest rooms of parade are on the second floor as they had been in the previous building. The baroque sense of drama is, however, heightened by this elongated progression to the most important rooms, the landing providing a convenient place to rest and consider the decoration.

The most spectacular feature is probably the staircase itself, which rises around three sides of the space, the steps appearing to be unsupported at their outer edge. Called a cantilevered staircase, this was a radical new feature of architecture at the time and was remarked upon for its ingenuity: 'There is another fine staircase, all stone and hangs on itself, on the outside, the support is from the wall and its own building, the stone of the half paces are large and one entire stone makes each', Celia Fiennes, 1697.

In the 19th century the stairs were found to have weakened and so cast iron beams were introduced at the outer edge of the steps, cleverly disguised with sculptural ornament. The gilded iron balustrade was wrought by Jean Tijou, the French master craftsman, who also created a magnificent gilded iron screen and gates at Hampton Court for William III.

Under the stairs stand two baby carriages and a child's sleigh. One is made to be pulled by a goat and the shafts are in the form of snakes, taken from the family coat of arms. It was probably used by the children of the 5th Duke and Duchess in the late 18th century. Beneath the window is a grey marble basin (1694) where the dishes from the nearby dining room were rinsed, and the doorcase is carved in alabaster from Staffordshire, demonstrating some of the many luxurious materials used in the construction of Chatsworth.

At the top of the stairs there is much evidence of the changing and developing taste of the 1st Duke. High up on the walls there are the remains of figural paintings in the same style as the ceiling by Antonio Verrio (1639–1707). They demonstrate that the Duke's original intention was to have a scheme of decoration similar to that in the Painted Hall. He subsequently changed his mind, however, and the three sculpted figures by Caius Gabriel Cibber (1630–1700) were brought in from the garden in 1692, and busts placed in the niches.

The ceiling depicts Cybele, the Goddess of Earth, in her chariot, symbolising Queen Mary, wife of William III. The cornucopia that spill coins over the cornice and down the wall indicate the prosperity that was expected during their reign. Cybele also appears in the central wall panel, with Ceres, Goddess of Agriculture, and Bacchus, God of Wine, each representing food and drink respectively. These wall paintings are executed *en grisaille*, in imitation of sculpture.

There are contemporary ceramics in the cabinet on the west wall. All of these objects were acquired by the present Duke and Duchess and demonstrate an area of their collecting taste, which continues to enrich Chatsworth and make it unique.

Recent additions to the collection include the sculpture *Carefree Man* by Allen Jones, in the centre of the room.

THE DUKE *writes*

The Duchess and I saw a 9 inch-high maquette for Carefree Man *during a visit to Allen Jones' studio in London to see some of his new paintings. A few months later, whilst Allen was staying with us, he agreed to make this much larger version for our Yorkshire garden. When we moved to Chatsworth we thought that this new site worked very well, and I am glad to say that Allen Jones agrees. Unintentionally, I believe, the figure looks very similar to the sculptor.*

Above: Detail of *Carefree Man*, bronze, by Allen Jones

BESS OF HARDWICK 400TH ANNIVERSARY
FIRST OF THREE SPECIAL DISPLAYS

The year 2008 marks the 400th anniversary of the death of Elizabeth Hardwick, who was responsible for creating the first palatial residence at Chatsworth. Universally known as Bess, she was born at Hardwick, to the east of Chesterfield, in 1521 or 1522. From a modest, respectable family, Bess eventually became the most powerful woman in the country after Queen Elizabeth I. Principally remembered as a fanatical builder of great houses, and an ambitious founder of aristocratic dynasties, her descendants numbered no fewer than three different dukedoms and one baronetcy.

Five monarchs ruled during her lifetime, beginning with Henry VIII and ending with James I. She saw the Dissolution of the Monasteries, the subsequent re-establishment of Roman Catholicism under Queen Mary I, and eventually the long and relatively peaceful reign of Elizabeth I.

During her long life – she was 86 when she died – she had four husbands. She married the first, Robert Barley, when she was 21 or 22. Unfortunately, Robert died a year later in 1544.

Top: Bess of Hardwick, oil on panel, *c.* 1560 (Hardwick Hall)
Above right: Henry VIII, 16th-century copy after Holbein's original of 1537
Above far right: Henry VIII's rosary, carved boxwood, Flemish, 16th century

They had met whilst in service to the Zouche family of Codnor Castle. It was an established tradition for children of the gentry to be sent away to serve in the households of wealthier, or better connected families, and learn how to be good courtiers.

Bess then became a waiting gentlewoman in the household of Lady Frances Grey, daughter of Henry VIII's sister. Bess became friends with her two young daughters, one of whom, Lady Jane Grey, would become the 'nine-day Queen'. Due to their royal status, the Grey family lived extravagantly and it was probably during this time that Bess developed her refined taste for lavish decoration and furnishings.

Made for Henry VIII in Flanders, one intricately carved object that is rarely seen at Chatsworth is Henry VIII's rosary (below). The largest bead bears the royal arms of England and inscriptions indicating that it was made during the King's first marriage to Queen Catherine of Aragon. This was before the Dissolution of the Monasteries, and Henry's break from the Church of Rome following his divorce from Queen Catherine. He then married Anne Boleyn, who was the mother of Elizabeth I. Henry was desperate to have a son, and beheaded Anne to marry his third wife, Jane Seymour.

In 1548, the first year of the young Edward VI's reign, Bess married her second husband, Sir William Cavendish. He was the Treasurer to the King's Chamber and, because of his position, she would have been presented at Court. During their ten-year marriage, they had eight children. William died in 1557. He had acquired a great deal of property during his employment as one of the King's commissioners, and ultimately had estates in several counties. The first five years of their marriage were based around their estate at Northaw in Hertfordshire but, in 1552, not long before the death of Edward VI, the Cavendishes sold their former monastic estates and concentrated their landholdings at Chatsworth. Here they began an ambitious building project, creating a grand house on two storeys.

Sir William St Loe, a landowner in Gloucestershire and Somerset, married Bess two years later. He was a Member of Parliament, and had been a commissioner at various inquiries for Henry VIII. He was present at the christening of King Edward VI, and was one of the official mourners at his funeral in 1553. The St Loe family was then involved in an attempt to place Lady Jane Grey on the throne. Sir William St Loe died in 1565 and, due to an estrangement with his brother, Bess inherited all his estates in the West Country.

Bess married George Talbot, Earl of Shrewsbury, in 1568. She had already witnessed one of the most politically turbulent periods of English history, but the events that happened next had the greatest impact on her life. In 1569, the Earl was appointed the official guard and jailer of Elizabeth I's cousin and heir, Mary Queen of Scots. During her long imprisonment, the Scottish Queen stayed at Chatsworth a number of times, in rooms that occupied this part of the Elizabethan house. The Earl was never fully reimbursed for the financial implications of this burden. Eventually, with increasing time spent

apart and his deteriorating health, and despite the intervention of Elizabeth I, the Shrewsburys' marriage broke down.

Above: Sir William Cavendish, by John Bettes the Elder, oil on panel, *c.* 1552
Below: Elizabethan Chatsworth from an embroidery, probably made by Bess

THE STATE ROOMS

The Great Chamber	The State Drawing Room	The State Music Room	The State Bedchamber	The State Closet

In 2006, these rooms were re-presented, to try and evoke a clearer sense of how they might have looked in the 17th and 18th centuries. They were the grandest rooms of the 1st Duke's building, and took the place of what was the Long Gallery in the Elizabethan house, which explains their unusual position here on the top floor. Apartments of state were intended principally for the reception of the King and Queen, and they derive their layout from the apartments in royal palaces in London and on the Continent. The progress of rooms, from the large 'Great Chamber' to the smaller but more important State Bedchamber and Closet, reflected the rigid and formal structure of life at Court. Access to the King or Queen was carefully controlled according to a person's status, with only a select handful of people gaining access to the most important private and intimate rooms.

Equally important, and carefully planned, were the views out of the windows and the relationship of the house to the 1st Duke's new garden. To the south was the Great Parterre, an elaborate pattern of flower beds, hedges, gravel paths and statues, as shown below in a detail from 1699. It was laid out in 1694 by London and Wise, who also worked for King William and Queen Mary at Hampton Court Palace. The sea horse fountain survives from that time. The Canal Pond beyond was dug for the 1st Duke later, to replace a hill that had obscured the view south. From the end window of the Great Chamber, looking east, the 1st Duke's guests looked out on a series of terraced gardens, with fountains, statues and parterres, and, above them, the Cascade, designed by a French engineer, Grillet, in 1703. Many of the most formal elements of this garden were simplified or grassed over as fashion changed in the 18th century.

26

Above left: Detail of limewood carving on the walls of the Great Chamber
Above: 17th- and 18th-century Chinese porcelain, on a cabinet in the State Drawing Room
Top right: Detail from the Mortlake tapestries in the State Drawing Room
Above right: Detail of the painted ceiling by Verrio in the Great Chamber

The State Apartment therefore was not designed for everyday occupancy by the householder, but instead as a space for parade, for entertaining and hosting the monarch. The lavishly carved woodwork, the dramatic painted ceilings, together with expensive tapestries, fashionable furniture, pictures and extraordinary silver-gilt plate, made a rich background for the ceremony of the Court. King William III and Queen Mary, who awarded the dukedom to the 4th Earl of Devonshire in 1694, and for whose possible visit these rooms were intended, never came to Chatsworth. It was not until the reign of Queen Victoria that a monarch visited Chatsworth, but she was entertained in the new rooms of the 6th Duke's North Wing.

The 6th Duke, in his *Handbook to Chatsworth* of 1845, says of the Great Chamber, which was known in the 19th and 20th centuries as the State Dining Room: 'It was never dined in that I know of – the first room of this great unappropriated apartment, which consumes in useless display the best habitable part of the house. What bedrooms might have been here with the south sun, and beautiful views! I was much tempted, but finished conservatively by repairing the sinking floors and threatening ceilings and, as a museum of old furniture and a walk in bad weather, I am well contented to retain this dismal, ponderous range of Hampton Court-like chambers'.

In the 20th century some of the State Rooms were used as bedrooms, although not as the 6th Duke would have imagined. Light levels in these rooms have to be carefully controlled, as it is essential that direct sunlight does not reach the furniture, tapestries, pictures and leather-covered walls, as it would hasten their deterioration.

THE GREAT CHAMBER

The first and largest of the second-floor State Rooms, and essentially unchanged since the 1st Duke's time, this was the principal room in which a visiting monarch and their Court met. They might also have eaten important meals here, although no record of any meals being served in this room survive.

The ceiling was painted in 1691–92 by Antonio Verrio (1639–1707), who also painted the ceiling over the Great Stairs. It depicts the *Return of the Golden Age*, with Vices destroyed by their opposing Virtues, a reference to the blessings of the reign of King William and Queen Mary. Interestingly, all the Vices appear at the eastern end of the room, furthest from the rest of the rooms in the sequence of the apartment, and therefore furthest from the monarch. One of the three Fates, Atropos (right of the fireplace) cutting the thread of life with her 'abhorred shears' is a portrait of Mrs Hackett, the 1st Duke's housekeeper, whom Verrio disliked. The mirror in line with, and the same size as, the communicating doors, was made to double the apparent length of these rooms when seen reflected from the opposite end, and to imply the presence of a second suite of rooms.

The limewood carvings on the oak-panelled walls are of fish, game-birds, fruit, flowers, foliage and draperies, carved (1692–94) by Samuel Watson, and by London carvers, Lobb and Davis, the team

of carvers engaged by the 1st Duke. Originally they might have appeared almost silver in colour against the darker background of oak, as limewood is a very pale timber. It has darkened and discoloured with time, so that today it is almost the same colour as its background. The window frames of this and the succeeding State Rooms were made in 1954 to match the originals which survive on the west front. They had been replaced with large plate-glass ordered by the 6th Duke in 1826, when it was new and highly fashionable. The new, individual panes of glass have bevelled edges and the frames are of oak from the park. The outside of the window frames on this side of the house are gilded, as they were for the 1st Duke.

The focal point of the Great Chamber is a buffet display of silver-gilt dishes. These date from the time of the 1st Duke of Devonshire and, like the porcelain on display, were intended to show the wealth and taste of their owner. The garlands of wax flowers and pyramid of artificial fruit were inspired by a contemporary painting by François Desportes in the Metropolitan Museum of Art. The fruit is based on that grown for the 1st Duke in his greenhouse, which stands in the rose garden today.

Above: Detail of Verrio's portrait of Mrs Hackett on the ceiling in the *Return of the Golden Age*

THE STATE DRAWING ROOM

This room was a withdrawing room, into which select members of the Court could progress from the Great Chamber. The ceiling, c. 1690, is by Louis Laguerre, and shows an Assembly of the Gods, with the Forge of Vulcan, and Vulcan discovering Mars and Venus, in the covings.

The tapestries were woven at the leading English manufactory of Mortlake in London c. 1635. They show scenes from the acts of the Apostles taken from cartoons by the Renaissance master, Raphael (1483–1520), which are now in the Victoria and Albert Museum. These were popular designs and several sets were commissioned by contemporaries of the 1st Duke. They were probably part of the original decoration of the room, but have lost their original borders and have been cut to fit the available space. Their rich colours have faded over the last 300 years. The present frames around them were introduced by the 6th Duke c. 1830.

The portrait over the fireplace is of Henry Clifford, 5th Earl of Cumberland (1591–1643), attributed to Daniel Mytens (c. 1590–c. 1647). The coffers and cabinet around the room are made from panels of coromandel lacquer, which first formed part of the wall decoration in the State Closet at the end of this suite of rooms. They represent another example of the 1st Duke's constantly evolving ideas for the decoration and furnishing of Chatsworth.

Crowded on top of the cabinets are examples of the superlative collection of Oriental porcelain at Chatsworth. Collecting ceramics, and in particular porcelain, was extremely popular. Porcelain was only made in the Orient before 1708 when the secret of its manufacture was eventually discovered in Europe at the Meissen factory, near Dresden in Germany. In the fireplace are examples of Dutch Delft urns, a tin-glazed earthenware decorated in blue and white in imitation of Oriental porcelain. Queen Mary was an avid collector of ceramics, the majority of which she displayed in special rooms at Kensington Palace, London.

The carved and gilded chairs were used by King George III and Queen Charlotte at their coronation in 1761 and were a perquisite (perk) of the 4th Duke's role as Lord Chamberlain. The upholstery is very rare, as it is still the original. The textile is woven with silver thread which has now tarnished and, on the backs, where it is protected from the light, the colours of the silks are still amazingly vibrant. The carpet is English, with a hand-knotted pile, of the late 18th century.

When war broke out in 1939, the buildings of Penrhos College, a girls' school in north Wales, were taken over by the Ministry of Food and the school moved to Chatsworth. The Painted Hall was used for assemblies and prayers, the Orangery became the art room, physics was done in the butler's pantry, biology in the still-room and chemistry, for safety's sake, in the stables. Dormitories were scattered throughout the house. Up to 20 girls slept in the State Drawing Room, shown in the painting above. The school left Chatsworth in 1946.

Top left: One of two coronation thrones of King George III and Queen Charlotte, carved and gilded by Katherine Naish and upholstered by Vile and Cobb, 1761

Top right: Coromandel lacquer cabinet, c. 1700

Above right: *Chatsworth in Wartime*, 1939, by Edward Halliday (1902–84)

THE STATE MUSIC ROOM

Formerly called the Ante-Chamber, or Green Velvet Room, this room takes its current name from the changes made by the 6th Duke. He inserted the central door on the north wall, displaying the violin door inside it, in 1836.

The painting of a violin on the inner door is a *trompe l'oeil* (meaning 'deceives the eye'). Even with close inspection, it is difficult to determine if it is real or not. It was painted by Jan van der Vaardt (c. 1653–1727), on a panel brought in the 18th century from Devonshire House in London (demolished 1924). For over 150 years, the violin has been one of the best remembered things by visitors to Chatsworth.

The stamped and gilded leather (*cuir repoussé*) wall hangings were ordered by the 6th Duke c. 1830 after he saw some at the château of Fontainebleau in France. In the frieze above there are nine portraits in leather of him, which he later regretted, thinking it too vain to have depicted himself in this way. Above the fireplace is a picture believed to be of the 2nd Duke

Above right: Detail of Van der Vaardt's painted violin
Left: *Portrait of the artist's daughter, Magdalena* by Cornelis de Vos (1585–1651)

when a young man, attributed to Mary Beale
(1633–99). To the left of the violin door is the large
Blind Belisarius Receiving Alms bought by the
3rd Earl of Burlington as a Van Dyck, but now
attributed to Luciano Borzone (1590–1645).
Lord Burlington also bought the painting *Acis and
Galatea* by Luca Giordano (1632–1705), and owned,
on the next wall, *The Procession of the Dogaressa
Grimani* by Andrea Vicentino (1539–1614).

The various pedestals and cabinets are by, or
in the manner of, the French cabinet maker
André-Charles Boulle (1642–1732). He worked
under the patronage of Louis XIV of France
(1638–1715), and was given workshops in
the Palace of the Louvre, Paris. They are veneered
with turtleshell, pewter and brass, a technique
synonymous with Boulle.

THE STATE BEDCHAMBER

The bedchamber, and the closet beyond, were the most important of the State Rooms. Access to them would have been rigidly controlled, to ensure that only a few senior courtiers and privileged guests were admitted into the King or Queen's presence. The room's status can be judged by the fact that the 1st Duke spent more on the furnishing of this room than any other in the house.

The ceiling, *c.* 1690, was painted by Laguerre. Appropriately for a bedroom, it depicts the Goddess Aurora (Dawn) chasing away the Goddess Diana (Night), identified by the small crescent moon on her head. The painted shadows in the covings appear to be cast by light from the windows, creating the illusion that it is morning.

The painting in the octagonal frame of *Venus and Adonis*, is attributed to Simon Vouet (1590–1649).

The original state bed ordered by the 1st Duke for this room was made by Francis Lapierre in 1697 at the then enormous cost of £470. It was the most expensive piece of furniture in the house, and was moved to Hardwick Hall, where its canopy can still be seen today. The present bed is dated *c.* 1700–10. It is probably the bed that the 4th Duke, as Lord Chamberlain, is known to have claimed as a perquisite (perk) after the death of King George II. A detailed examination in 2005 revealed that it had been cut down by 47 cm (18.5 in) at some point in its history. It was decided to raise the top frame to its original height, levelling the hangings and revealing the feet covered in silk damask. As the most important piece of furniture in the house, it was always

Below: Detail of Laguerre's ceiling painting

intended to have a towering presence. The silk damask upholstery is original to the bed, apart from a new section on the bedhead which was woven in 2005. This new silk was also used to make new curtains.

The large mirror, decorated with the arms of the 1st Duke and Duchess, was made in 1703 by John Gumley (active 1694–1729) and cost £100. It is an extremely rare example, being signed and dated by John Gumley in the centre of the lowest section of glass. Another mirror can be seen in the closet next door. In the winter of 1998–99 both were dismantled, conserved and restored and many missing pins and fragments of glass replaced.

The silver-gilt toilet service on the dressing table is the most important silver toilet service in western Europe, being the oldest and most complete example of Parisian silver known to have survived. Silver was often melted down and made into something more fashionable as tastes changed, or simply used to raise capital during times of crisis or war. The latter happened very frequently in France as a direct result of Louis XIV's many military campaigns. The service, made in 1669–71, is decorated with the arms and monogram of William

of Orange and Mary (later King William III and Queen Mary II) and is likely to have been a gift to Mary to celebrate their marriage in 1677. It was probably given to Mary, Countess of Devonshire, wife of the 4th Earl and future 1st Duke, in recognition of her husband's support of William in the 1688 revolution. Toilet services were used during the morning ritual of the 'levée', which could last several hours, during which the lady would receive visitors.

The silver perfume burner near the fireplace is attributed to Philip Rollos and dated to the 1690s. It is made in three parts: base, vase and lid. The vase is pierced to allow clouds of perfumed smoke to escape and scent the air. The lid is topped with a flame, to represent the burning incense tablet inside. Incense in the time of the 1st Duke included expensive naturally occurring ingredients such as stag's musk and verdigris from the sperm whale.

King George V and Queen Mary were the first and only monarchs to sleep in this bedroom when they stayed at Chatsworth for the Royal Show at Derby in 1933. It was also used by members of the family at Christmas until the Second World War.

Above: View into the State Closet,
with Simon Vouet's *Allegory of
Peace* above the toilet service
Left: Silver-gilt toilet service
1669–71, and 1678

THE STATE CLOSET

This is the smallest and most private of the five State Rooms; no-one would have entered without the express invitation of the King or Queen, and it is where they could conduct their most private, personal or state business. The room was later referred to as the Dressing Room. The ceiling, c. 1690, again by Laguerre, depicts the legendary beauty contest between Juno, Venus and Minerva, sending Mercury – the messenger of the Gods – in search of Paris who would judge who was the most beautiful of the three.

Originally there would have been no chandelier: it was hung here by Duchess Evelyn in the early 20th century. It is one of the few surviving pieces of silver furniture in this country, and is decorated with putti on each of the branches, each supporting an Earl's coronet. Above this, there is a larger putto who holds aloft a Ducal coronet. It probably marks the elevation of the 4th Earl of Devonshire to the Dukedom in 1694.

The fireplace was added in 1912, based on one of an appropriate date at Hampton Court. It is decorated with a massed, staged arrangement of porcelain. There is also a large amount of Oriental porcelain displayed on the walls, hung in pendants.

A trend for decorating rooms with clusters of ceramics began in Europe in the 17th century. Queen Mary established this in England: no space was left unfilled, above and below furniture, on top of chimney-pieces and suspended from the walls. Porcelain was yet to be made in Europe and held great allure for the western world. In an attempt to copy Oriental porcelain, factories in Europe covered earthenware with white tin-glaze and decorated it with enamel colours. The blue and white pyramids in this room, made to hold cut flowers, were produced in Delft in the Netherlands in the 1690s and were highly fashionable.

By the time of her death in 1608, and as a result of her four successive marriages, Bess had acquired, inherited and amassed a great number of estates up and down the country. The focus of her attentions had always been Chatsworth. Then, in 1583, when her marriage to the Earl of Shrewsbury finally collapsed, she purchased from the executors of her brother James's estate, her parental home at Hardwick. When she left Chatsworth she took as many of the lavish furnishings as she could, and set up her new home in the now-ruined Old Hall. Bess began to alter and aggrandise the house until, in 1590, her estranged husband died.

Almost immediately, she set about creating a new building close to the old one. She employed the fashionable architect, Robert Smythson, who had worked for the Earl at Worksop Manor. Smythson's design for Hardwick was extremely novel, with no internal courtyard, a tradition that originated in medieval defensive architecture. Instead, all the rooms are outward looking, with vast windows, enabling them to have extensive views across the estate. Although still unfinished, in 1597 Bess finally moved into her new house. Each of its six towers is crowned with a stone frieze bearing her initials 'ES', proclaiming to everyone who was responsible for creating this extraordinary new building, complete with a magnificent High Great Chamber intended to receive the monarch.

In the last years of her life there were disagreements between Bess's children. These were aggravated when, on her death in 1608, it became clear that her favourite son, William, now Lord Cavendish, was her chief heir. William was the most sensible of her children, and had made the most of the money and opportunities he had been given by their mother. She was clearly rewarding his behaviour in the hope that it would ensure the security of her legacy for the future.

Fifty-five years old when his mother died, William inherited exceptional estates. He commissioned a pictorial survey of them by William Senior (right). Bess had chosen what she bought with a keen eye for income, and her son was now able to add to it by further investment. In 1609, William bought back the Chatsworth estate from his brother Henry, who had inherited it from the Earl of Shrewsbury, thereby reuniting Bess's two principal building achievements. In 1618, William was made 1st Earl of Devonshire by King James I. This reputedly cost him £10,000, but he could afford it: by 1620–21 his total income came to £24,000, mostly from rents, but including £5,000 from the sale of wool, £843 from cattle, and £1,000 from the East India Company, in which he had invested.

Left: Hardwick Hall
Right: Chatsworth, from William Senior's survey of 1617

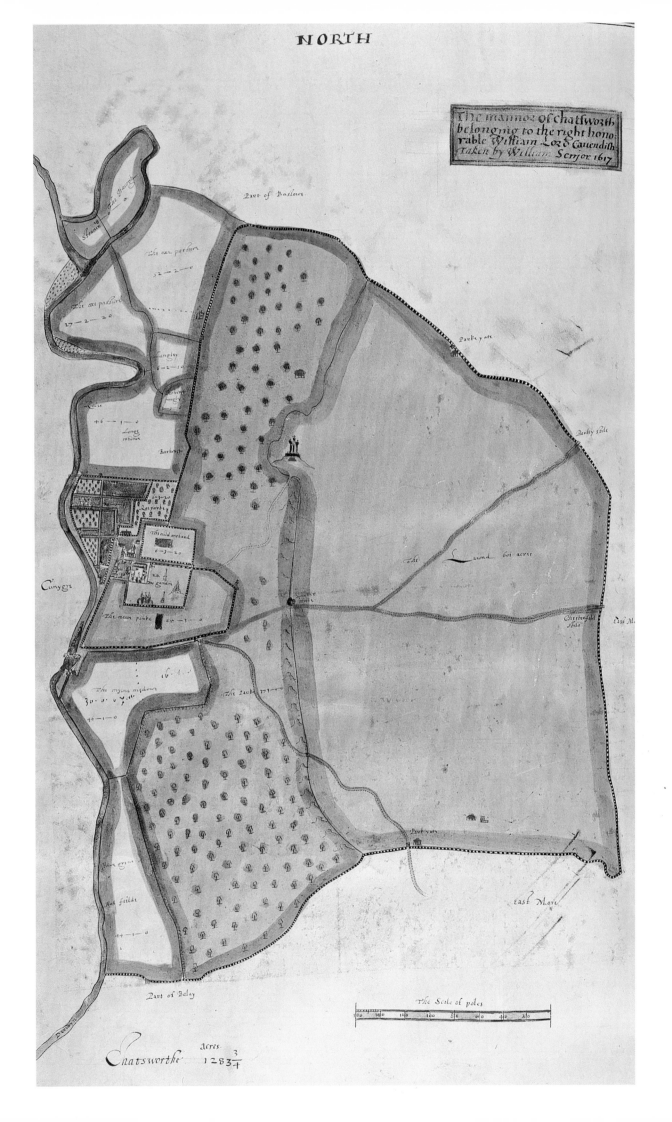

The mannor of Chatsworth belonging to the right honorable William Lord Cavendish taken by William Senior 1617

Part of Baslow

The oxe pasture
52-2-0

The oxe pasture
27-2-20

Langley

Reas
46-1-0

Longe medow

Bar̄hurst

Cunyger

The mill orchard
6-7-20

The new parke 29-7-0

The myne medow
30-0-0
40-1-0

The Lecke

Parke yate

Barley stile

The Lawnd 601 acres

Chestrefeld stile   East M.

Parke yate

East More

Part of Belay

Chatsworthe   Acres
12 83 3/4

The Scale of poles
160 140 120 100 80 60 40 20

THE SKETCH GALLERIES

The Sketch Galleries were added by Wyatville for the 6th Duke in the 1830s to improve circulation around the house. They were originally used to display Old Master drawings, or sketches, from the collection. These were removed to storage for their protection away from direct light, and the galleries currently display a variety of other objects from the collection. In 2009 they will be re-opened with new permanent displays from the rich and diverse collection of paintings, furniture, photographs and decorative art, many of which are not currently on view. In addition, the blanked-off windows into the courtyard will be visible. In the west gallery are family portraits spanning 12 generations, together with photographs of the present Duke and Duchess and their family.

Top left: The Duke and Duchess, 2007

Top right; Lord and Lady Burlington at an estate party to celebrate their marriage in 2007

Above left: The 12th Duke of Devonshire, b.1944, by Tai-Shan Schierenberg, 1997

Above centre: The Duchess of Devonshire, b.1944, by Michael Leonard, b.1933

Above right: The Earl of Burlington, b.1969, by Tai-Shan Schierenberg, 1999

THE WEST STAIRS

The doorways on all three floors were originally windows giving directly onto the court, providing more light than there is now. They lead to corridors which, like the Sketch Galleries, were added by the 6th Duke to make it easier to move round the house. The wrought iron panels on the landings are by Jean Tijou and incorporate the initials C (Cavendish) and D (Devonshire) with Ducal coronets. They were originally made for the Great Stairs, but were later incorporated into the balustrade, which was made by the local smith, John Gardom, in 1702. The ceiling depicts *The Fall of Phaeton*, and is one of the earliest examples of Sir James Thornhill's (1676–1734) work. In the winter of 1998–99, it was cleaned and restored.

On the first floor, the carved stone tablet showing the names and dates of the Dukes of Devonshire was completed by John Lane, stonemason at Hardwick Hall. *Samson and Delilah* by Tintoretto (1518–94) is on the wall of the last flight of steps.

At the bottom of the stairs on the right are two celebrated paintings. The iconic portrait of *Georgiana, Duchess of Devonshire* by Thomas Gainsborough (1728–88) was stolen in 1876 after having made a world-record price at auction, but was only acquired by the Chatsworth House Trust in 1994. To its right is Sir Edwin Landseer's *Trial by Jury*, or *Laying Down the Law*, of 1840, a canine satire on the legal profession, and Court of Chancery in particular. On acquiring the painting, the dog-loving 6th Duke had Landseer add his Blenheim spaniel 'Bony' (to the left of the French poodle) as a cub reporter.

THE WEST CORRIDOR

On the left as you enter the corridor is an Egyptian stele, or memorial tablet, from the 11th Dynasty (dateable to 2134–2040 BC) and, on the right is another, smaller one from the 12th Dynasty (dateable to 1991–1782 BC). The mutilated marble torso is from the Holy Land and dates from the late 12th century, a rare example from the 'Crusader' period. The stalactites under the table of Derbyshire fossil-limestone are from Castleton, 14 miles (22.5 km) away.

Across the courtyard, you get the best view of the trophies carved in stone by Watson and the connecting galleries designed by Wyatville, which were added on the other three sides in the 19th century. Samuel Watson from Heanor, Derbyshire, came to Chatsworth in 1689 and worked here, in wood and stone, almost continuously, until his death in 1715.

The 1st Duke's fountain in the courtyard was restored to use in 1973 after having been a flower bed for many years. It originally had a statue of Arion, which is now in front of the 1st Duke's greenhouse in the garden.

In the courtyard, you can also see five bronze dogs by Nicola Hicks, (born 1960).

THE DUKE writes

I joined the Board of Sotheby's in 1994, and three years later these greyhounds by Nicola Hicks were put up for auction with us. I had been aware of this artist for quite a time, but being able to see these sculptures in the gallery for a week or so before the sale made me very enthusiastic indeed about her work, and particularly these dogs. We acquired the dogs, and they went up to our garden at Bolton Abbey in Yorkshire, where we were then living. There they remained happily until we moved here in 2006. These bronzes are more fragile than they look and so putting them in the courtyard where everybody can see them, and yet nobody can be tempted to sit on them or pull at the tails, is an ideal solution. The artist says that they can be arranged however we like and we do move them around the courtyard from time to time.

On the wall is a new acquisition by the Duke and Duchess, a painting of the *Emperor Fountain* by Tarka Kings.

THE DUKE *writes*

Tarka Kings came to Chatsworth to paint a tree, a commission by our son, William Burlington, and whilst she was doing this, she spent some time painting the Emperor Fountain, initially as a diversion from her main task. She enjoyed this subject and has been back on several occasions, sometimes for two or three days, to paint the fountain at different times of year.

As we had come to know Tarka quite well during her visits, she kindly asked us to her studio to preview her solo exhibition, before it opened at The Fine Art Society on Bond Street, London, in November 2007. We were thus able to acquire this wonderful big study of the Emperor Fountain within its immediate surroundings, as well as a number of smaller works which are not currently on display. We were impressed by her treatment of the surface water, and the atmospheric feel of the whole work. I hope that she will return to work here again next summer.

Between the windows hangs a major work by Lucian Freud (born 1922), *Skewbald Mare*, 2004. The viewer immediately notices the lack of the horse's head in the painting; the artist explained that he had thought the head weak and wished to concentrate on its tactile flank and rump.

At the end of the corridor is a painting by Sean Scully (born 1945), *Wall of Light; Red Day Leaving*.

THE DUKE *writes*

My parents have known Lucian Freud since the early 1950s and my father had collected and commissioned work from him for over 50 years, but the credit for the acquisition of this painting must go to my mother. When in London, she often visits Lucian Freud and therefore sees whatever he is working on. Thus, in 2003 and 2004, she became well aware of this painting as a work-in-progress, and the more she saw it, the more she fell in love with it. Even before Lucian Freud's exhibition in the Wallace Collection, she had persuaded my father and me that this painting was worthy of the rest of the Freuds in the collection and so we were able to acquire the work before the exhibition opened. The horse, called Sioux, is cared for by Sister Mary Joy. She looks after several horses which are ridden by disabled and disadvantaged children living near Wormwood Scrubs in west London. Lucian has painted the horse several times, taking his paints and the canvas to the stable to work from life.

THE DUKE *writes*

We were in Fort Worth, Texas, for the Breeders' Cup race meeting in 2005, and we saw a group of Scully's works in the Museum of Modern Art there, which amazed and excited us: we then spent months discussing the possibility of acquiring a new work by this artist with his gallery, Timothy Taylor: this is the result. This work was not a commission, but I think that Sean Scully is happy with the way this work is displayed here.

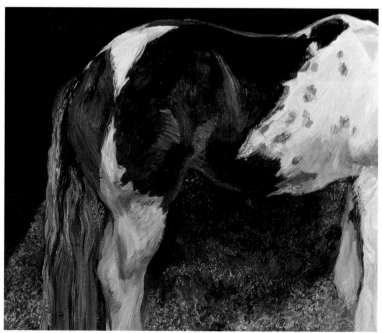

THE CHAPEL

The chapel was built between 1688 and 1693 and has remained unaltered ever since. If the 1st Duke could return to Chatsworth, he would immediately recognise his creation. The Duke had his own chaplain, who would have led prayers for the household here, staff sitting downstairs and the family using the richly decorated gallery above. Laguerre and Ricard painted the walls and ceilings with scenes from the life of Christ, and Verrio painted *Doubting Thomas* over the altar. Samuel Watson and a team from London carved the altar-piece of local alabaster. The two large flanking figures of Faith and Justice were executed by Cibber, who designed the whole. The limewood carvings on the walls are by

Samuel Watson (1662–1715) and partners, not by Grinling Gibbons as sometimes thought, and the original design drawings for them survive in the collection (see detail, left).

The four black marble columns were hewn from a single block quarried on Sheldon Moor, a few kilometres away. The strong smell comes from the cedar wainscot, and not from incense as often thought. The pair of huge brass candlesticks was bought for £60 in London in 1691.

The sister of the 11th Duke, Lady Anne Cavendish, was married in the chapel to Mr Michael Tree in 1949. In 2007, the present Duke and Duchess's fifth grandchild, Cosmo Dunne, was christened here.

Ceiling with painting showing Christ in Glory, by Louis Laguerre (1663–1721)

47

BESS OF HARDWICK 400TH ANNIVERSARY
THIRD OF THREE SPECIAL DISPLAYS

Bess of Hardwick died at Hardwick on 13 February 1608. During the last five years of her life, she hardly travelled, and the people who visited her noted that she was becoming increasingly frail. As time went on, her son William increasingly took responsibility for the management of her estates and financial affairs and, in the last few weeks, he spent most of his time by his mother's side. As her condition worsened, her mind was constantly preoccupied with all her affairs of varying importance. She began to instruct William with additional bequests and last wishes which he dutifully added to her will. For the last eleven days of her life, she was constantly attended by a doctor and, on the day of her death, her three surviving children were gathered round her.

Her status as a Countess dictated that her funeral was arranged and conducted on heraldic lines by the Garter King of Arms of the College of Heralds. This process took time (in Bess's case nearly three months) and, therefore, her body had to be embalmed. Five days after her death, her body was transferred to All Saints, Derby, (later Derby Cathedral), and placed in the family vault awaiting the funeral. The College of Arms organised the service and one of their tasks was to ensure that the interior of the church was covered in black cloth. Enormous quantities of black cloth of differing quality were also ordered to clothe the servants and family. Exotic foodstuffs for the funeral feast were gathered in London and shipped north.

The funeral finally took place at All Saints, on 4 May 1608. The procession entered the church headed by a mourning knight bearing a banner painted with Bess's coat of arms, followed by official heralds. At the end of the sombre procession were her servants, a number of poor folk from the Shrewsbury almshouses and 58 mourning women. Bess was interred in the vault under the elaborate monument designed by Robert Smythson. The monument had been finished as early as 27 April 1601, and 'wanted nothing but setting up'.

Design by Robert Smythson for Bess of Hardwick's monument in All Saints Church, Derby

THE OAK ROOM

The oak panelling and carved heads which decorate this room are from a German monastery and were bought by the 6th Duke on an impulse, having been tempted into an auction room in Berners Street, London. Inset into the panelling between the windows are paintings of some of the 6th Duke's favourite dogs. Ten other paintings in the panelling are records of his holidays and were returned to this room in 2001, after an absence of nearly a century. They are by John Wilson Carmichael (1800–68) of views of Cullercoats near Newcastle, except two which are of Naples and by Raffaele Carelli (1795–1864).

The 6th Duke gave his own account (1845) of the various uses to which this room was put: 'It was the dormitory of poor Dicky Smith, the Chaplain; and to this room I remember banishing the learned Parr, when he insisted on having a room to smoke in – a desire then (1813) considered most atrocious and derogatory. Of late years, when family prayers have been read, this has been the suitable place for them; and when the Grand Duke Michael Paulowitsch arrived on a visit last year at a very late hour here he had the gayest-looking supper which contrasted agreeably with the dingy walls, and looked like a jolly friar's repast'.

Before it was altered, this room contained some of the 12,000 volumes of the library of Henry Cavendish (1731–1810), the scientist. The opening from the chapel was made in 1960, to ease the circulation of visitors. Many of the smaller pieces of Oriental porcelain and ceramics in the collection are in the cupboards round the room.

Above right: Henry Cavendish (1731–1810) grandson of the 2nd Duke
Left: An Italian torchère, walnut, late 17th century, in the form of a winged figure of Atlas, supporting a Victorian bracket clock by John Smith of Derby

THE CHAPEL CORRIDOR

The Oak Room leads back to the Chapel Corridor. The two ancient Egyptian statues of the goddess Sekhmet were moved here from the garden in 1991. They come from the temple of Mut at Karnak and date from the 18th Dynasty (1386–1349 BC). The colossal foot (below), long thought to be a 19th-century fake, has now been identified as part of a gigantic Greek statue, dating from the time of Christ. The other foot is in a Berlin museum.

The paintings of Chatsworth on the south wall show how it changed over the years after the 1st Duke's house was completed in the early 1700s. The most marked change prior to the building of the new North Wing in the 19th century can be seen in the landscape, undertaken for the 4th Duke in the 1760s by Lancelot 'Capability' Brown.

The group of porcelain vessels in the fireplaces and along the corridor was made by Edmund de Waal in 2006–7. Commissioned for Chatsworth by the Duke and Duchess, de Waal was influenced both by his conversations with them and by porcelain already at Chatsworth. When you look closely, you can see the vessels are covered with blue and grey glazes, some shiny and others matt. The large, white, lidded jars in the fireplaces (bottom right) echo the Dutch Delft earthenware (right) similarly displayed in the State Apartment, thus linking the 17th century and the present day.

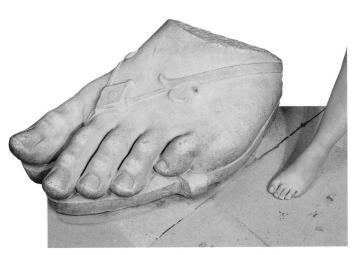

THE DUKE *writes*

We met Edmund de Waal through Joanna Bird, who is an inspired and inspiring dealer in contemporary ceramics. I was given my first piece, a small bowl by John Spearman, about eight years ago, which came from Joanna's gallery in Chiswick and, since then, I have become more and more interested in contemporary ceramics and she has been an excellent guide. Initially, I was attracted by the coolness of Edmund's work, having only seen a few of his smaller pieces, but then he had a large show at Blackwell in the Lake District in 2005 which opened my eyes to the possibility of him doing some sort of site-specific installation here at Chatsworth.

Edmund came to Chatsworth several times to try various ideas in different rooms, but eventually we all decided that it would be better to start afresh and this is the stunning result. The making of the large pots particularly is very technically difficult and they are a huge physical achievement from that point of view alone. To have these wonderful pieces, Edmund has described them as a 'cargo' of pots, filling one side of this stony passage is very intriguing. There are subtle differences in the glazes, both of colour and of texture, so they never look the same: the play of light and shade at different times of day and at night all add a mystery to this space, but also they are individually and collectively just beautiful objects.

THE GROTTO

The Grotto supports the Great Stairs above. It was originally conceived to contain the lowest flight of stairs, but these were eventually built in the Painted Hall. The bas-relief of *Diana Bathing* above the fountain on the south wall was bought in 1692. Its marble frame and basin below it, the swags of flowers in Roche Abbey stone and the Garter Stars in the ceiling, were all carved by Samuel Watson. The fountain was made to work again in winter 1999–2000 and the stonework of the walls and sculpture were conserved in the winter of 2002–03.

In the middle of the room is a steel sculpture by Sir Anthony Caro, *Table Piece XCIV*, 1969.

THE DUCHESS *writes*

I have lived with this sculpture since I went with my mother to buy it, nearly 40 years ago, and it is still my favourite piece. I like it because of its great simplicity and uncomplicated design. It gives me a feeling of calm and tranquillity, yet it also has a feeling of strength; perhaps some of this comes from the contrast of the grey steel against the white plinth.

In his early career in this country, Caro worked with Henry Moore in a figurative style. In 1969, when he made this piece, Caro had just moved to America, and started to use large sheets of steel, which he had not been able to acquire in England because of the shortage of steel as a long-term result of the war. When I walk past, I always give it an extra glance because I am fascinated by how something so simple can look so different from each angle. I would really like to see it on a plinth that rotates very slowly, with a strong light from above, so that you can see it from every angle. The next best thing is to place it in the middle of the room, so you can walk all round it.

To the left of the fountain is a Carrara marble sculpture by Tim Harrisson (b. 1952), *Sheaf of Light*, 2004. He also carved the two smaller limestone pieces on the table called *Across the Edge*

On the wall is a new painting by Endellion Lycett-Green, *Portrait of my mother*.

THE DUKE *writes*

Endellion Lycett-Green's parents, Rupert and Candida, are very old friends of ours and therefore we have been aware of her career as an artist right from the beginning. Stupidly, I missed the opening day of her first, and so far only, solo show in London and, by the time I viewed it, two days later, every single work had been sold, so we have had to wait for about three years until she produced another work which became available to us.

I am glad that we waited, as I think that this is a really outstandingly beautiful work. It is called Portrait of my Mother, *and the plants, mostly hellebores and euphorbias, are Candida's favourites.*

Delli Lycett-Green does not produce very much finished work, but everything of hers that I have seen has been extraordinarily beautiful and I think that we are lucky to have this painting of hers here at Chatsworth.

Anthony Caro, 1995, photographed by Jorge Lewinski

THE OAK STAIRS

This staircase was built by Wyatville in 1823–24 to give access to his new wing, begun in 1818. The dome and lantern were completed in 1829, currently concealed by a later inner dome. It was installed in 1928 for the 9th Duke, and designed by the architect W. H. Romaine-Walker. They attempted to disguise Wyatville's work as that of the time of William and Mary by putting in old doors and adding surrounds and a cornice in the style of the 17th century. The brown brocade and stippled walls (plaster painted to look like stone) also date from 1928. The chandelier of stags' horns was originally in the Theatre and was hung here in 1959.

The large equestrian portrait of William, Lord Cavendish, later 4th Earl and 1st Duke, is by an unidentified artist, possibly French

Right: *A man in oriental costume*, Rembrandt van Rijn (1606–1669)

or Flemish, *c.* 1675. Lord Cavendish had accompanied an embassy to France and is shown dressed in the height of French fashion.

The portrait by Sir George Hayter of the 6th Duke was given to the 11th Duke by Derby Borough Council when their Guildhall became a theatre in the 1970s. Opposite is a portrait of King George IV from the studio of Sir Thomas Lawrence (1769–1830).

The 6th Duke brought the important Rembrandt van Rijn (1606–1669), *A man in oriental costume*, from Devonshire House, London, where it had hung since the 3rd Duke had acquired it in 1742. It had formerly been in the collection of Cardinal Mazarin. The identification of the subject of the painting, generally dated 1639, has raised much scholarly debate but no satisfactory solution has yet been found.

THE LIBRARY

Originally this room was the 1st Duke's Long Gallery. The ceiling of gilded stucco by Edward Goudge, with paintings by Verrio, survives from this time and its design is reflected in the Axminster carpet which was woven when the room was altered.

In 1815, the 6th Duke fitted the room out as a library. He bought several complete collections of books to add to the many he inherited and he and Wyatville designed the present gallery and bookcases to receive them, c. 1830, which is also when the cut-velvet curtains were hung. Some of the furnishings were originally made for Devonshire House, Piccadilly. In 1983, the paintwork and gilding of the Library were restored. On the table to the right of the door is a small easel painting, a still-life by Renoir.

Top: *The Library, c.* 1827, watercolour by William Henry Hunt (1790–1864)

55

There are over 17,000 volumes in here and in the Ante Library. A large private library such as this, purchased and inherited by successive generations of the Devonshire family, consists of many different elements. In addition to printed books and manuscripts of the past six centuries, in many languages and on every subject, it includes most of the autograph writings of Thomas Hobbes, the philosopher, and Henry Cavendish, the scientist, as well as important groups of political and family correspondence. Originally the Old Master drawings and prints were also part of the Library, where they were kept in splendid albums. Because of their fragility, it is not usually possible to display delicate works on paper. However, treasures from the Library and archive are frequently lent to exhibitions around the world, and can be studied here, by prior arrangement, by scholars working on particular projects.

Page from *A Book of Hours, According to the Use of Sarum (Salisbury)*, an illuminated manuscript on vellum, Flemish, *c.* 1500. This book belonged to the 4th Duke's father-in-law, the 3rd Earl of Burlington. It is a prayer book originally given by King Henry VII to his daughter Queen Margaret of Scotland. As well as the painted miniatures illustrating the life of the Virgin, the borders are painted with illusionistic flowers, birds and insects.

Drawing by Raphael (1483–1520), *Woman reading to a Child*, *c.* 1512. Purchased by the 2nd Duke, who formed one of the world's finest collections of drawings and prints, this was a preparatory study for a painting. Such drawings, though not usually intended as finished works of art, were highly prized by artists and connoisseurs alike.

Illustration from one of the four volumes of *The Birds of America* by John James Audubon (1785–1851), purchased by the 7th Duke. It is one of the largest, and certainly the most famous, of all bird books, and contains life-size, hand-coloured engravings based on drawings of 1,065 birds in their natural habitat.

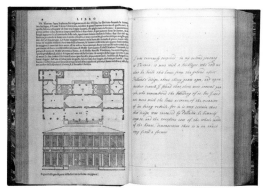

Page from a volume of the *Quattro Libri dell'Architectura*, 1570, by the Italian architect Andrea Palladio (1508–1580). This was one of the most prized possessions of the 3rd Earl of Burlington and it contains his hand-written annotations in the margins, made while viewing Palladio's buildings in northern Italy.

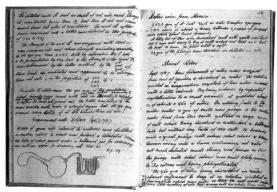

Pages from a notebook of Henry Cavendish (1731–1810). A grandson of the 2nd Duke, he was a great experimental scientist, who determined the composition of water, recognised hydrogen as an element and was said to have been 'the first man to weigh the world'.

THE ANTE LIBRARY

Ceiling painting by Sir George Hayter (1792–1871)
Right: Crystal found during the making of the
Simplon Pass

The Ante Library contains some of the thousands of books to be found throughout the house. The bookcases are made of mahogany and brass like those in the Library. Among the books in these two rooms are those that belonged to the renowned scientist, Henry Cavendish, a grandson of the 2nd Duke. The ceiling painting was the Royal Academy's picture of the year in 1823, *Venus supported by Iris complaining to Mars*, by Sir George Hayter (1792–1871).

THE DOME ROOM

This is where the 1st Duke's house ends and the 6th Duke's North Wing, built 1820–28, begins. The two vases are made of a very rare marble, *occhio di paone*, and are the first of many examples in this part of the house of the 6th Duke's passion for stone.

The central bronze sculpture (above) is a copy of the famous *Mercury* by Giambologna. It was moved here recently from the Great Stairs' Landing, but was originally positioned by the 6th Duke in a room that is not open to visitors.

Daniel Fisher made the Flame Bowl on the table in the window by hanging it from a turntable and stretching it into shape. Raised in Norfolk, his interest in light perfectly suits the porcelain of this bowl, which is stretched until it is so fine that it is almost transparent. The Duke placed the bowl in front of the window in the Dome Room to demonstrate how easily natural light passes through the torn porcelain rim.

THE GREAT DINING ROOM

So-called to distinguish it from the Great Chamber, or State Dining Room, and three other dining rooms in the house, this is the first important room of Wyatville's wing. When it was finished in 1832, the 6th Duke wrote: 'It answers perfectly, never feeling overlarge… It is like dining in a great trunk and you expect the lid to open'. It was used by the family until 1939 and redecorated and hung with crimson material in 1996.

The four heavy gilt pier tables were made for the room. The glass lights on the wall, from Devonshire House, London, were put up here in 1959, having been in packing cases for 40 years. The marble fireplaces and bacchanalian figures were carved by Richard Westmacott the younger (1799–1872) and Robert Sievier (1794–1865). The 6th Duke was disappointed with them; 'I wanted more abandon and joyous expression', he wrote.

The first dinner given in this room was for Princess (later Queen) Victoria when she stayed here with her mother, the Duchess of Kent, in 1832. The Princess was 13 and it was the first time she dined with adults. There was a cooked rehearsal the night before. Most of the large pieces of silver, commissioned by the 6th Duke for use at banquets, are by Paul Storr (1771–1844) and Robert Garrard (1793–1881).

The portraits to the left and right of the door as you enter are of *Arthur Goodwin* (1639) and *Jeanne de Blois* (c. 1635) by Sir Anthony van Dyck (1599–1641). Between the fireplaces is *Christian Bruce, widow of the 2nd Earl of Devonshire, and her children* by Daniel Mytens (c. 1590 – before 1648). The portraits on the right of the fireplaces are of the 3rd Earl and his wife, also by Van Dyck.

On the table left of the far door are vases made of Blue John, the Derbyshire fluorspar mined only in this county and first worked by the Romans.

Above: A dinner for King Edward VII and Queen Alexandria, early 20th century
Left: *Arthur Goodwin* by Sir Anthony Van Dyck (1599–1641)
Right: One of the Blue John vases illuminated from the inside

THE VESTIBULE AND MUSIC GALLERY

The Kitchen, c. 1832, by William Henry Hunt, 1790–1864)

Now you pass through the vestibule. Food from the kitchen was brought through the door on the right and kept warm on heated tables in the alcove on the left. The gallery above was where the 6th Duke's private orchestra played and, in later years, the band for the annual staff party. The two Indian statues of Jain deities came from a temple in the state of Gujarat, and the 6th Duke bought the Burmese Buddha in London.

The watercolour of the 6th Duke's kitchen in the North Wing, was painted *c.* 1832 by William Hunt. From here, successive head cooks and their kitchen and scullery maids provided food for the family and their guests in the dining room, the children in the nursery and the staff in the servants' hall. Around it were sculleries and vegetable preparation rooms, a room for confectionery, a meat larder, dairy, ice safe and a plucking room. The head butler and his staff were responsible for the preparation of the dining table and the serving of food and drink. The kitchen was used until the late 1940s; it is now the joiner's workshop, and can be seen on a pre-booked, behind-the-scenes tour.

THE SCULPTURE GALLERY

The 6th Duke indulged his love of stone and sculpted figures in this room, which he built to display his collection of what was then modern sculpture. The artists he consulted recommended the plain gristone walls as a perfect backdrop for the top-lit marble sculptures. On the left as you enter is *Discobolus*, by Matthaus Kessels (1784–1836). *The Spinning Girl*, of 1819, is by Rudolf Schadow (1786–1822), *The Wounded Achilles* by Filippo Albacini (1777–1858) and *A Veiled Vestal Virgin of 1847* by Raffaelle Monti (1818–81). On the right is *Mars Restrained by Cupid* by John Gibson (1786–1866), *Ganymede and the Eagle of Jove* by Adamo Tadolini (1788–1868), *Hebe, Cup-bearer to the Gods* and *The Sleeping Endymion with his Dog* by Antonio Canova (1757–1822).

For the group of Mars and Cupid, Gibson needed an exceptionally large block of the best Carrara marble, which was finally delivered to his studio in Rome drawn by 20 buffaloes and with 'the whole town out to watch'. The round bas-reliefs on the walls are *Day* on the right and *Night* opposite, by Bertel Thorvaldsen (*c.* 1770–1844).

Above: Neoclassical sculpture: Antonio Canova's *Hebe* (left) and Adamo Tadolini's *Ganymede and the Eagle of Jove* (right)

The rectangular reliefs on the right depicting scenes from the legend of Achilles are by the same sculptor, and those on the left, by Schadow, show rape and battle scenes from the story of Castor and Pollux.

In the middle of the gallery, Napoleon's sister, *Princess Pauline Borghese*, by Thomas Campbell (1790–1858), and his mother, by Canova (bought in 1818), sit in their white marble chairs. These and *Endymion* were among the most treasured purchases of the 6th Duke: he admired Canova above all other sculptors. Later in the 19th century these works went out of fashion. Now they are sought-after once more and a major exhibition of neoclassical art in London in 1972 put them back in the public eye so that they are now considered amongst the most important works of art in the collection.

In 1990, eight more pieces of sculpture were returned to the Sculpture Gallery, from whence they had been removed at various times during the previous 80 years. The group of *Paris and Oenone*, 1848, in the centre of the gallery is by Ludwig

Michael von Schwanthaler (1802–48), who called it his swansong because it was the last work he completed before he died. In the central bay on the right (east) wall are two recumbent figures, *A Bacchante* by Lorenzo Bartolini (1777–1850), commissioned by the Duke in 1822, and *Venus with Cupid removing a thorn from her foot*, 1825, by Pietro Tenerani (1789–1869). On the left (west) wall is *The Cymbal Player*, 1832, by Richard Westmacott the younger (1799–1872).

The two massive lions either side of the door to the Orangery were the bulkiest removals. They are copies of those by Canova which form part of the Rezzonico Monument in St Peter's, Rome.

Left: *A Veiled Vestal Virgin of 1847* by Raffaelle Monti (detail)
Above: *Crouching Lion* by Francesco Benaglia (detail)
Below: A 19th-century photograph of the gallery

The Sleeping Lion is by Rinaldo Rinaldi (1793–1873) and the Crouching Lion which weighs 3.5 tons (3.6 tonnes) is by Francesco Benaglia. They were commissioned by the 6th Duke in 1823. For many years they were outdoors, flanking the steps from the Orangery into the garden. Now they are back in their original positions. The busts in the niches, high up each side of the door, are of Canova by Rinaldo Rinaldi (1793–1873) and The 6th Duke, by Thomas Campbell. Nearby, against the right (east) wall, is another copy of Canova's work,

a bronze statue of The Penitent Magdalen.

The gasoliers, now electrified, were bought from Wanstead in Essex when the contents of that house were sold in 1822. The doorstops are sawn-off models of Joseph Paxton's Great Conservatory, which formerly stood in the garden.

Above: The Sleeping Endymion with his Dog by Antonio Canova with The Wounded Achilles by Filippo Albacini in the background

THE ORANGERY AND OTHER SHOPS

The 6th Duke's plan for the North Wing was to end with the Sculpture Gallery, but when he got 'bit by gardening' due to the enthusiasm engendered by his head gardener and friend, Joseph Paxton (1803–65), the Orangery was added. More sculpture and tender plants shared it happily for years. Now it contains a shop, but there is still room for a copy by Lorenzo Bartolini (1777–1850) of the Medici vase and several remaining marble busts and statues by neoclassical sculptors.

When the house re-opened in 1949, guidebooks and the sickly-sweet Chatsworth bon-bons, sold from a wheelbarrow, were all that were offered for sale. By the 1960s, part of the Orangery had been arranged as a shop and the range began to grow. Today you can see a wide variety of gifts, many inspired by designs from the house, collection and garden. In 2008 the shop is also offering a new range of contemporary craft pieces. The profits go towards the upkeep of the house and estate.

Here ends the tour of the house. You have walked around a third of a mile (0.5 km) and have climbed 100 steps up and 60 steps down since you went through the gates of the lodge. From the shop, you now enter the garden, which has its own guidebook. If you want to leave the garden to eat or shop at the stables, or visit the Farmyard, your ticket will allow re-admission to the garden today.

The farm shop in Pilsley, a village 1.5 miles (2.4 km) from Chatsworth, opened in 1977 and is long established as one of the finest food shops in the country. Focusing initially on Chatsworth produce, such as meat, game, dairy products and potatoes, the shop then expanded with its own bakery and delicatessen, and now sells a huge range of the best British food and wines. There is a popular café with beautiful views over the estate. In 2008, the shop has been refitted and expanded, and innovations include a fresh fish counter and plant sales. The shop hosts food tastings, talks and demonstrations throughout the year; please contact Lizzie Greaves on 01246 565300 for details.

The five gift shops, in the Orangery, Stables and Farmyard, sell products that reflect the quality, beauty and diversity of the house, collection, garden and estate. Many items are designed exclusively for us. The garden shop in the stables sells home-grown plants, fruit and vegetables in season, garden furniture and other gardening essentials. Our new Chatsworth interiors shop in the stables sells items for the home.

THE GARDEN

The garden covers more than 105 acres (42.5 hectares) and there are several miles of footpaths to explore, as well as the famous waterworks, a growing collection of sculpture, the maze, Joseph Paxton's rock garden, the Grotto and Pinetum and the rose, cottage, kitchen and sensory gardens. This year, a long-overgrown part of the garden, called Quebec, has been opened up, to

Detail from an early 18th-century view of Chatsworth, by Tillemans, showing the recently uncovered Cascade, right

reveal new views into the park, and a 300-year-old Cascade, left, which appears in early paintings of the garden. The gravity-fed waterworks play every day, subject to rainfall.

The fully illustrated 64-page garden guidebook contains maps and trails that help you find your way around, and which highlight particular features and themes. All parts of the garden are described, and a history section looks at the layers of the garden's history, the important gardeners who have worked here and the many other influences that have gone into creating this landscape over 450 years.

THE PARK

The park was largely laid out by Lancelot 'Capability' Brown in the 1760s. It has always been a farmed, food-producing landscape; the grass is grazed by sheep, cattle and deer; the river provides fish and the woods, game and timber. Most of the park is open free throughout the year, and visitors are welcome to walk, to bring their

children and dogs, picnic and play games. Every year we stage events in the park, including the International Horse Trials in May and the three-day Country Fair. There are also walks through Stand Wood, behind the house, with spectacular views over the house and valley.

In 2008, Queen Mary's Bower (above), a surviving viewing platform from the Elizabethan water gardens, is open to visitors.

SCULPTURE

Sculpture has been a feature of the landscape at Chatsworth for more than 300 years. In recent years, important contemporary sculptures, a particular interest of the Duke and Duchess, have been added to the garden and park at Chatsworth. The *Lying Down Horse* by Dame Elisabeth Frink has finally found its resting place off the Arboretum Walk, close to the Grotto. Frink's *War Horse* currently dominates the stables' courtyard, and in 2002, the Chatsworth House Trust bought another Frink sculpture, *Walking Madonna*, which is placed in the garden, 109 yards (100 metres) south of the top garden entrance. More sculptures from the family's collection will be placed in the garden over the year. The garden also hosts temporary sculpture displays, including selling exhibitions of contemporary sculpture, and visitors can expect to see a fascinating range of work over the course of each year.

In 2008, two newly commissioned site-specific sculptures are being placed permanently in the garden. *Déjeuner sur l'herbe*, by Allen Jones, features three figures in a clearing beyond the Canal Pond; the other new work, by David Nash, is made for the Pinetum at the far end of the garden.

With the return of International Horse Trials to Chatsworth in 1999, the Duke and Duchess commissioned a series of new sculptures that can also be used as jumps during the two days of the Trials, by artists such as Tim Harrisson, Alison Crowther and Nigel Ross, and these can be seen in the park to the north of the house.

Top: *Pegasus*, 2002, by Tim Harrisson
Far Left: *Male figure*, 1988, by William Turnbull
Left: *Lion Woman*, 1999, by Emily Young

Clockwise from top left: *Walking Madonna, c.* 1981,
by Elisabeth Frink; *Lying Down Horse*, 1972,
by Elisabeth Frink; *The Two Graces*, 2000,
by Allen Jones; *Epona's Leap*, 2005, by Nigel Ross;
2 column jump, 2004, by David Nash

STABLES AND FOOD

The Carriage House restaurant is in the beautiful stables, built by James Paine in the 1760s. Recently redecorated by the Duchess of Devonshire, it currently displays a series of new paintings of Chatsworth by Kitty North. During the season, the restaurant serves more than 20,000 people each month, and a number of weddings and other private and charitable events take place there during the year. The catering department also runs the newly refitted Cavendish rooms, and other food outlets in the garden, car park and Farmyard. In the stables there is also a suite of reception rooms available for weddings and other special events. Further details can be found on our website at www.chatsworth.org.

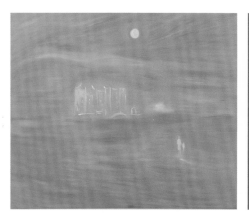

Above: Three paintings of Chatsworth from the series by Kitty North, on display in the Carriage House restaurant, recently added to the collection by the Duke and Duchess

THE FARMYARD

The Farmyard was opened in 1973 and, in 2003 welcomed its three millionth visitor. It was designed to offer an entertaining but non-sentimental way of explaining the life cycles and uses of the ordinary commercial farm stock on the estate. Throughout the season there is a varied programme of activities and demonstrations, animal handling sessions and a daily milking demonstration in the afternoon. The Farmyard also welcomes school and student visits, which offer young people an insight into food and farming on the estate. The woodland adventure playground is one of the largest in the country and, as well as the usual slides, chutes and swings, has two water play areas which draw their water from the stream. The café and gift shop have been completely refitted for 2008.

From the Farmyard or the house entrance, we also run the popular 28-seat Discovery Trailer, which takes tours through Stand Wood above the house and round the lakes, and through the park. The trailer is fully accessible for wheelchair users, and seats are sold on a first-come, first-served basis. Please ask for times of rides each day.

EDUCATION

Chatsworth welcomes thousands of young people every year, as part of our extensive education programme in the house, garden, farmyard and park. Chatsworth provides unique surroundings in which children can broaden their knowledge and understanding of the curriculum,

and many schools and colleges produce exceptional work inspired by the estate, from film, literature and art, to animal husbandry, career development and tourism projects.

Recent work by students at Wilsthorpe Business and Enterprise College

ESTATE AND ACCOMMODATION

Chatsworth is the centre of a 35,000 acre (14,164 hectare) estate, encompassing farms, woods, moorland, rivers, villages including over 400 dwellings, quarries and other industries, both large and small. All the businesses, both in-hand and tenanted, that make up the Derbyshire estate, including as far afield as Buxton and Bolsover, are administered from the Estate Office, an 18th-century brick building on the edge of the park, originally built as a hotel for visitors to Chatsworth.

There is a wide variety of superb self-catering holiday accommodation on the Chatsworth estate. Ranging from the Hunting Tower and Swiss Cottage on the hill behind the house, to converted

farm buildings at Manifold and Wetton, they all offer a unique atmosphere and warmth of welcome. For details of all the self-catering accommodation on the estate, please telephone 01246 565379.

The Devonshire Arms in Beeley is a traditional pub with a twist; the contemporary restaurant serves exceptional food in a colourful and vibrant atmosphere, and this style extends to the eight double rooms, offering exclusive B & B. Telephone 01629 733259 for further information. On the edge of the park is the elegant 18th-century Cavendish Hotel at Baslow, with 23 bedrooms, telephone 01246 582311. Also on the estate is the Shottle Hall Country House Hotel, telephone 01773 550577.

Other beautiful places to visit

BOLTON ABBEY
Skipton, North Yorkshire

Since 1753, the Cavendish family, and now the family Trust, has owned the Bolton Abbey estate in the Yorkshire Dales National Park. The ruins of the 12th-century priory are situated in an outstandingly beautiful position overlooking the River Wharfe, surrounded by some of the most spectacular scenery in England. Telephone: 01756 718009. www.boltonabbey.com

There are two hotels belonging to Bolton Abbey, the Devonshire Arms Country House Hotel and the Devonshire Fell. Visit www.devonshirehotels.co.uk

LISMORE CASTLE
and Lismore Castle Arts,
County Waterford, Ireland

The Cavendish family has an Irish home, Lismore Castle in County Waterford, situated in the Blackwater Valley, in one of the most delightful parts of Ireland. The magnificent walled gardens are open to visitors from Easter until October. In a wing of the castle, Lord Burlington has led the creation of Lismore Castle Arts, a spectacular contemporary art space, which holds annual exhibitions and hosts a series of events and programmes linked to the displays. For further information on opening times for Lismore Castle Arts, the garden and renting the Castle please telephone +353 (0)58 54424, www.lismorecastle.com and www.lismorecastlearts.ie

72